T0312910

chromatic

defacement

chromatic

defacement

Phillip Foss

chax press / tucson 1998

The poems in this volume have appeared in the following publications: *The Carrionflower Writ* (Melbourne), *Conjunctions, Denver Quarterly, Notus, o-blek, screens and tasted parallels, Sulfur,* and *Temblor.* Th title of the poem "Speech Runes . . ." is from *The Lay of Sigrdrifa.*

This book has been manufactured in the USA by McNaughton & Gunn, Inc., in Ann Arbor, Michigan.

Designed & published by
Chax Press
101 W. Sixth Street, no. 6
Tucson, Arizona 857-1000
USA

ISBN 0-925904-17-1

Library of Congress Cataloging-in-Publication Data

Foss, Phillip.
    Chromatic defacement / Phillip Foss.
       p.   cm.
    ISBN 0-925904-22-8   (alk. paper)
    I. Title.
PS3556.O755C48   1998
811'54--dc21   98-21402
                                                        CIP

for

Carlos Ruiz-Lolas

Mark Spencer

and Sergio Moyano

This thing called light is itself transparent,

but it apparently changes into something non-transparent.

— Kobo Abe

Table of Contents

The Theater of Perfumes

When did we three last meet?

— Samuel Beckett, etc.

The floor slopes toward the stage as if
to encourage liquids, or airs, directionally.

With a snake's tongue you desire to smell.

The room is glazed black, its ceiling
excessively high, as in a theater, but
there are no chairs for an assumed audience.

The confluence of her thighs is an exit.
Navigation must, by design, exist in absence
of signs. You have approached innocence
by inhaling between her breasts, to thus
condescend to suffocation.

He has swallowed a crystal of quartz; heart
illuminated with dialogue.

She is reclining on a scarlet bed, which
tastes of iron or blood. You contemplate
the imminent nuisances, delights.

You cannot understand the language she is
speaking and, while her red lips move,
the sound seems to emanate from her palm.

The stage is so distant the actors' voices
reach him only after bouncing off the black.

There are apparently miles between you and
her, as if you were a raptor.

You can smell her breath.

Many different languages are involved
in the feigned dispute. He knows none, yet
from attitude concludes they are concerned
with the absence of music.

They are dragging about a monkey's head;
presumably a symbol.

You are drinking her cologne.

When she glances at you, her irises are red.

Prop: a helmet with mirrors
in the eye sockets.

With mascara she has drawn eyelashes
on her forehead; the attendant irises are red.

There is a monkey's body on the bed.

When they turn out the lights he imagines
he can smell the person who would be sitting
next to him.

She is in the process of translation;
assumes the position of a clairvoyant.

You are crying because their voices continue
in issuance; hearing another conversation
as the tears strike.

When she covers her eyes with her palms
you read the future.

The monkey is leashed, balanced on an actor's
head. The soliloquy issues from its mouth.

.

This is the audition, so you are blindfolded.
Your palms are secured to your face
with cords. Your nostrils are scorched.
You are prepared.

The first note is ammonia; the second,
licorice; the third, cedar.

It is dissonant.

The fifth is cinnamon; sixth, heather;
seventh, vinegar:

cacophony.

Eighth: pigweed; ninth: ice; tenth: burnt
hair; eleventh: coal; offal; pine; coffee;
fifteenth: blood; sixteenth: cod; seventeenth:
cherry blossom; tobacco; nineteenth: leather.

You are becoming nauseated;
the future is iris.

.

          : To contain emotion one must
willfully denounce any attempt at appropriation of symbols
of transgression.

          : There are long fine filaments
extending from the pupils which do not distort vision
and which can only be perceived, by another, if the subject
is positioned correctly in conceivable light.

          : The paradox is to orchestrate
the perfumes to prevent arbitrary mingling, mutation
or conversance, other than prescribed by score.
There can be no improvisation.

          : Once grown, the mask
cannot be removed, but like a snake shedding its skin, faces peel
off revealing an endless succession — continuing to grow
from the core.

                  :   Ideally, a female actor
mouths the words, while a hidden male enunciates them.

                :   To alter emotion, alter
color, and if the subject is composed of glass its moods
are endless. The ideal instance is a glass ball floating
in water within a bowl fabricated from mirrors.

                :   The music must continually
repudiate its own aspirations, its own desire.

                :   Predictably, the structure
of the body must be destroyed, so that all movement
is antithetical to natural predilection.

                :   Any other conception
would fail to repudiate the conventions prescribed by chaos.

•

She is floating naked in snow. There is an aura
melted around her. As if for sustenance,
her mouth is open.

You can see yourself seated on the horizon.
You are cutting the alphabet
into your fingertips.

The accumulating snow is causing his face
to become masklike; the left side sags
as if from stroke.

He is speaking from the right side
of his face; thus he is lying, in profile.

You have evolved the equation
that his speech makes you snowblind.
This allows you to extend your arms to touch
her with your fingertips.

She believes that touch is contagion;
your tendencies in perception
remaining on her skin.

You are transcribing his dictation;
the words drop as small globes of ice
from the left corner of his mouth.

She is seeking to become transparent; glass
or ice, so that her waist will break light.

She has designed this transformation
by memorizing the angles of the flakes
which fall into her mouth.

From where you sit, you perceive this
as the inversion of speech, or as consumption,
thus filling her with articulation.

He sees her fingers move rhythmically
and believes she is hearing music, her fingers
in sympathy, but she is counting.

She is barely floating above the damp ground,
so her pale shadow is askance.

Thus the skin of her back and buttocks
is not distorted by pressure.

You would like to insert your hand
in that space, in sympathy with absence.

Because of the temperature in absence,
there is no odor which he could rub between his fingers.

.

No set.

8 followed by 34 by 67 by 2 by 6 & 39, double duration by 110 less 4 by 99 held to end.

First voice:

What is the duration of resonance

What is the duration of yellow

What is the duration of decline

What is the duration of trajectory

What is the duration of rose

What is the duration of cloud

What is the duration of appetite

Second voice in simultaneity:

The taste of a voice

Absence captured in one's mouth

The anonymity of nakedness

The tongue as hand

Light as passivity

To structure on the basis of mutation

Killing as the cessation of a perfume

The composition is based on the notion of walking
down a crowded street with one's eyes closed, and smelling

the various perfumes of women which pass by. The intent
is to discern her in this seeming cacophony.

And thereby possess her by assimilation
of her perfume into your body.

·

She is lying on a pane of glass.

He is opening small vials of perfume.

You are in the audience, anonymous.

The pane is suspended three feet
above the stage.

He is pouring the perfumes, with delicacy
and precision, upon her.

She is grasping a flame, as if self-
immolation were a metaphor.

The ascending vapors form
a visible fog above her.

This she waves goodbye to you.

But to your tongue the air is but appetite:
the soprano's breath.

·

The entrances to the perfumes are oblique, are lacunas,
are dismissal of time, are metronome.

There is the entrance of apology. Therein, even if singing,
one's voice is retracted into one's mouth as if one were
consuming a rodent in the manner of a snake.

From this entrance one cannot ascertain conversation
since perspective is consumptive, not sympathetic.

The texture of one's voice is prescriptively coarse.

There is the entrance of appetite. This too is consumptive,
but here there can be no apology or satiation.
Neither is the entrance of desire. The absences are similar,
glass to obsidian, perhaps twins which speak
mutually unintelligible languages.

Surface here is that of the tongue, not palate.

Hue is invented as pink, or yellow.

There is the entrance of lace. One does not enter here,
though it is a curtain. To enter would be to rend the fabric;
one must merely look through, and thus enter by eyes
and passion, so the body is exiled from this form of hearing.

Hue must be white, as absence, a design of nothing
which overlays a texture of regulation over that which one desires.

The texture is that of hair; fragrance
that of slightly overripe fruit.

There is the entrance of submission. The opening
is very low, or very shallow, as if its fabricator desired removal
of one's head in entering, not concerning stature
but sensation and dialectics.

The perfumes must be symphonic, harmonic, absent
of individuation, like a mob or flock which moves
with synchronicity and endorsement of history.

The taste is sulfurous; the texture of pitch.
There is the entrance of predation. Its orifice is a metaphor,

beak or jaw. Its voice is a tole: an odor of warm entrails;
an equation of subtraction to compel accretion, as one rolls
a ball of snow.

This must be falsetto and frenzy.

A game of blood-dots in snow; the loser, clothing.

To enter here one must carry the arms of malice
and of dispersal, techniques of absorption.

There is the entrance of conceit; there is the entrance
of cruelty; the entrance of promiscuity; of delight;

pathos;

obstacle;

the numinous;

excretion;

abandonment;

there is the entrance of absolution, vindication,
and the entrance of volition.

She assumes herself as this perfume, as these perfumes,
yet possesses no exit by which to enter.

The Doubt Teleologies

Is there anything which is this or something else, which is permanent or impermanent, which is both permanent and impermanent, or which is neither?

— Nargarjuna

Petite bliss. Dice to release. Accretion is erosion. To vaporize
the body with gasoline: sleight.

The equation of desire or a landscape of desire? In the palm,
can apology, a feather, be as light? Weight is spectrum.

Beatitudinal dissolution: breath inhaled behind one's head;
to inverse perspective, deaccelerate into fraction: heart.

Fingers as relics, nostalgia. Coy annihilation, the mineral
is enjoying, tasting, the mineral. Unchance in trajectory.

Does darkness anticipate the vehicle? Darkness is vehicle.
To then anticipate: the hand shaking itself: incest.

Reticent: a series of O's passing through each other as matrix,
intercourse; the numerology, passion without object.

Within the shadow is a darker shadow; this is the use of hope,
none of which, necessarily, is a perceptual door, or anchor.

An issue of architecture, the ground mutating; architectural
equilibrium, gravity or vertigo, residencia of deceit.

The habitation, watercolor (here the spectrum remains arbitrary),
and temporality of action enamoured within decay.

At shifting light, feverish virtuosity, playing the imagined
score: invasion, or translation, faith.

Problematic notation: empirical flux. Or vicarious appetite
as sublime transcendentalism.

A collapse into insomnia, the dreaming then ill, a condition
of helmets, or indifference.

This invents a causal structure, casual structure, both
internally and externally enveloping space, or introversion.

The stick as morse code delimiting the parameters of unperceived
territoriality; water questioned as auditory impairment.

Trance or venial sin; the purity mutations. Gesticulating
furiously like a dying bird: sign language to the transparent.

Is walking rapidly then conversation, ideate conversion,
where the landscape is a synchronistic set?

Merely people, abrupted from temporal linearity into a coquettish
effluvium of desire: exile the mind.

In articulation can it then be corrupted, killed by nascent
momentum, or achieve a jurisdiction compelled by meandering?

The percussive is tantamount to reprieve, an epistle of air,
sonorous declaration, missive truncation.

Fear: condition of black lines, the individual feinting
toward vapor.

These structures are endemic, like whorl, or wave,
to then regard as thine, in entreaty.

The crossed jurisdiction of tactility and vision is responsive
for eloquence? No commitment to homogenous voice.

A sudden slap of air distorts linear trajectory: a desire
to hear glass; the desire not to touch eyes.

Transcendence into landscape has created encagement by music:
topography inverted by sleight of eye.

Release the mechanism of extroversion, so face is appropriated
by painting, desire as stasis, lust.

Then one: defacement; no responsibility to glamour, virtue,
merely cognizance of what is in mutability.

Purgatory, comedy: personality dismemberment: ballistics
of concentration propelling vacuity: heart no longer feels.

Invention of inspection, or introspection: fire confined by mirror,
or footfalls forever arriving, departing: metronome.

Metronome: heart, fluid redundance: tapdrum, sunset,
hoofbeats: counterpoint; no music within dance.

The self in history. A mistake: contrived explanations
for plausibility. This is satisfying, the nuisance of volition.

Progression of decline: erotic bouquet, waves dropping
off the end of the earth, a sensibility.

All the iridescent wings, and the blindfolding music,
like an apology for thrust, the plenitude of debris.

Intimate structure of doubt, brothel, suffocation; the storm,
banal mythos, and the beauties under erosion.

All fragrance, the problem. The scalp bleeding with worry
and the masks put away until the next final fear.

Accelerated duration or radius of desire:
what then is the distance to release?

Capricci 25

The left side of my face harbors a vacuum, as if breathing
were involuntary, an escape from persuasion, relation,
or tendency toward oratory

My spine achieves a vibrancy as of bells where the barest
excess is an excuse for concealment of cherished notion,
like tactility; the way lips open to scream; numbers

My accent makes me gag, or the odor of walnut is a sphere
of confinement, either is a rook, either a medal of desertion

Friends: you are sick, you are diseased, you are perverted
Let us part without emotion: a transparent membrane
hoods your faces; I am reluctant to lick your hands

in fear of salt

sign language

The corners of your mouths are ripped from the exertion
of language: each tooth inlaid with an ebony letter

My musical notations are physics: b-flat & c-flat = light

My hearing is damaged

There is no left side to my face; it has been removed
by pressure; the cheekpiece is a vacuum: my profile
diffused by sound

When I play, my skeleton is a resonator: propaganda

My penis is the bow; as if breeding were involuntary

Landscape is involuntary, an excuse for failure or bosom

the nipple is salty

nursing is signing

Thus the violin is a weapon

I desire a weapon of grace, purity, finality: I have holes
in both ear drums which could represent the entrance
and exit holes of a bullet, but which do not

disease

or perhaps music; in any case I cannot hear words
of women whose waists mimic violins

The reverse cannot be true

A violin with breasts; imagine the playing — but I fear
the salt — imagine the sound: an ascension, numbers
collecting, collecting, collecting. Against erosion

Such wishes

Everything is a weapon: caprice destroyed my nervous system;
labia disturbed my levitation; gravity destroyed my speech

I have found that god is reduced to an equation: ballistics,
velocity, notation, geometry, genetics, b-flat

altitude?

The bell proves you are submissive

When I hold the violin to my cheek the notes secreted
from the holes fill my nostrils with hope

Sea stretches indefinitely, by appearance, and who is to question
that? The line of its horizon could be perceived
as a violin string

Imagine the percussion; imagine percussion:
the cheapest form of thought

Easy release is seldom available, given the disclosures
of erosion; given the way things levitate and exceed optics

Once I killed myself observing stone; such weight was in my
head I surrendered to song, though I have no voice

or I have been disemboweled by sight

The sight of the world must be reconciled to an equation
of sound (or wound); sound to emotion; emotion to genitals

Does a soprano crescendo equal orgasm

No, it is a weapon; a hollow spine, embodied,
though the reverse cannot be true

since sound comes off the gut as light through a prism
and penetrates the heads of the assembled — or so they believe —

but if I play: there is no world, they believe I am absent;
if I play: there is *a* world, they believe I am

Thus I acknowledge just debt:

Vinland

Conceal the bones in throwing.   False face.

Forests of starvation,   sullen, and impersonated gems
As excuse for excursion   a drunken land.

A new moon, a new taste,   transformed tongue
Mute. Compulsion,   the horizon infinite,

The dead, objects. Gathered   against the years
Are brief exclamations   of transcendence, or torque,

Exquisite defacement   into landscape, all bark,
Textural reticence. Defilement   through chance;

The soil sucks up the body,   politely. Guest.
Solstice as punishment for moons.   Dreamt, melded, seen:

Stone stone, word word,   blue red.
Anxiety drought, draught,   mudhole and vermin: version

Of sky, bobbing clouds   underfoot, shattering.
Blue heron wing bone whistles   eaten silently.

Coax widgeon, aloof of play,   water plane, skip.
Airscape of then token coins   in ascension as targets.

Candidates of the spurious;   amputated hands.
Plot of magic,   crown to torment vision.

Such delusion,
Of the emotive:

Rut, sundown sleep, wine dream.
Hasp locking the lips

The star
Of blood

the universe cancelled
ox and cart, rut,

Never again
against mirth.

of paradise but a burst
in the head.

Incessantly murmuring gods.
The cataloging of despairs: micaceous ruins.

Incised in the skin of succulents.
Instrumentation of fear, berating

In the forlorn steps.
The peeling skin synonymous

Trail to vanquish.
Quilled tongue as honor and respite

Of midnight air,
Rapiers of intent

Grasping, imprimatur of arrest,
Into dry palms,

All then sleep,
Of consciousness;

Helmet of hair.
And horoscopes

Bowstring of nerves;
rock after rock

An adrenaline of pain,
with redundant bells.

Predaceous sleep,
from decadent wet

such singing. Eternal despair,
hands mitigate against

as a griffin,
the honor to kill.

as synchronistic rebuttal
the hoof is idle,

Mane cropped. Ascent out   of unknowing land,
Lust and accord,   into transmigration of soul

Or stone, time displaced,   place dismembered, fragments
Of representation,   graffiti against a pure

White, pure vacuity,   pure concession to unknowable
Design: white on white,   black on black, the scripture

Braille, eyes   plucked, fingers
Sheared.

In defacing moonlight,   it is a vinolent erection,
A sympathy   of nightmare and shadow;

Every minute is contained   by law and the atmosphere
Suffocates with souls.   There is no escape

As the pedantic: all have been judged
Guilty and rivers   are disguised as white

Effluvium. Without exertion,   descent is possible
To whatever sea is posited as escape,   as release,

There is no clarified;   there is no detached.
Only intoxication   from observing mutation,

Mutation as it plods   though the order
Of every enchantment,   every disenchantment,

And ends only as end.   No rhapsody, nostalgic context,
Only objects, living or not,   residing in proximity

To sensation. The door opens   here, cannot reopen,
Cannot be reopened, closed;   closed to beginning over,

Knowing. No, no matter   how lush, it is always desert,
Opaque, an infinite pane of glass   bisecting the head

At the elevation of the eyes.   An enticement, incitement,
Inverted, poet's throat cut,   and the boats falling

Off the edge. To where,   there is nowhere
To swim, finally, no isle   of relief, no shore

Of opulence, no rest.   The only refuge is in assigning
Random value to the participants   in identity:

Ocean is dog is snowflake is love is not, as yet,   lost
To the mere momentum of moving   to an other, other

Than the known. A gift, perhaps,   in the form of sound
In intercourse   with the greater drone of air

Grinding down the topographies   of faces.
A gift.   Perhaps.

Slough of sky, clumsy mirror of ice: the romantic
Disinterment of selves . . .   (This world will never be,

Nor will to be: manes to be sea spray;
Holiness pursed lips   extending wind;

Or the book of feathers,
Gravity be your god.)

or the book of butterfly wings:
Trail, trough, the steps

Of timidity always in descent,
Toward. The sun

always in ascent,
sets in the face, the gates

Open and close endlessly,
Concealing and revealing

a great eyelid
an empty socket, seer.

So then the world becomes white,
Cloud; becomes a waterfall

becomes mist,
covetous of cakes

And portions of beasts;
An alphabet; voice

becomes voice speaking
directing the hand

Translating the speaking weapon.
Must come purgation.

To they must come manner.
To they

Must come repentance: stride,
And brain safe

stride, stride; skull
within the helmet of faith —

Incantations seared
For the sky

into the scalp
to reap.

All nether land rapport,
What chance articulation,

hope in what chance light,
chance intervention?

Before the fluent
Then as word?

what fragrance is worn
What strident posture

Assumed in silhouette or sleep?
From the recourse

What self emerges
of sentience?

Bag and bead, quirt and rod,
Fleshes fused,

the season is misplaced,
the future has spun

Back behind. A gyroscope,
Or transcendence, top. Gone

of trance
then the opulent excess,

Caliber of quest only
Over air, the voices minute

an armor sheathed
winds exchanging

Like brief birds
Indictments of topography

relaxing from a fist into ten
or its lack.

To go where then?
What impassioned eye? Aggrieved

In what shout,
the idea, idyllic

Cessation of history,
Tool, taste, or marriage

defilement of the consecrated
of structures. Gone.

The Pleiades. Judgement.
Gull swirls away,

Off the side the sea
always away. Always

Nether; never is it in hand
It is abutment of will,

like a grim toy.
stone or sea

Against which to toil
And collapse. The drift

in unrequited caste. Collapse
drifts; rive

Runs. Cast up the eyes,
Heaven does open:

cast up the hands:
the forehead under serration.

The world is seized.
The world is bestowed.

The world is intoxicated.

What hands?
What hands?

Purgatory

Often then, foam against intent;
traces of behavior throughout. Silent
impassioning. Cactus squall, mud
astronomy and the circuit of walk. Sky
table or diminished stature of
observation, of compulsion. Bereaved
image, and the crucified piety about
sand. Sad legions toward lava, mists of
hell, ascension. Chalice, chromium
tongue, siege of grass; the mask beard.
Hope, hope, hope, conceal, oh, then in
praise. Such water. Beneath and before
the murder: tremolo of revenge, of
remorse, carnage-carrion. Care. Bound,
then, burden, mute lip and divine
impersonation: goat. Shiv and shank,
serrated teeth and touch. To speak out
against defilement: the trading of milk.
Chance winds and destiny deaths. The
apologies of lust: porpoise and whale
fused. Man fused man: aplurality,
disguise, and vindication. Hallowed
tongue, come as materialism. But with
one eye the future is mindless.
Proliferation of breasts, innocence
debated back. Assigned to killing as art,
a broken boat. Not a drunken boat,
linearity. Pure white bark, defacement.
Denude. The accumulated pain, holly and
mistletoe. Chance birth, chance stars,
extant hand. Time to reprehension, crown
of gems, elevation. Running birds and
the proposal of floods as measurement,
elevation. Astringent savor and the
calligraphy, decree of plain. Some same
abutment as claustrophobia; chanson of
maneuver or hover as monologue of wine.
Tariffs of the host: quotation of chance
or salamander. Such luster and the
horizon but whimsy, but demarcation of

mind or arbitrary caution: an antiphony.
Then a vocabulary of fools that indicts
smiles or at least a reciprocity of
knives. Caution the harmonies so
resplendent of ash, the fig tree, the
lime. It is the mirages of hubris which
foster your fragrance. Such slow faith,
reticence, or remorse at all that is
lost or forsaken or replaced by caprice.
Like time. Abrupt those inferences of
devotion, the fashion of decline. Beaten
beyond the attributes of concession is
the frail resonance, the sign of bird or
song. The argument is for cadence. Or,
at least, apostles of the ordinary,
scant light. Climates of debt; the
sleight. The passions are severed in
choreography or congress. A cycle of
indifference. All survive in quixotic
affirmation. Confirmation. Pyrography
of flesh; scansion, or a partial opal. What
light can, will go away, as, perhaps,
papyrus, or rush, as race is thicker than
thought. Is there then a parallel gesture
of dismissal? Recalcitrant bout? Why to
always be lesser than the ornamental
corpse? Caste lips absolve. Hideous
vocalizations of those obliquely ecstatic
equal the heinous preservation of that or
such. It is all faith (sweet indelicacy).
The agenda precludes mesmerizing snakes
and dancing or the purchase of salvation.
Artificial bodies in display as flesh-
emotive, as a chronicle of that which
was when linearity approved, as earbones,
as a geology of sacrilege: oxbow;
refraction of apology. The blackened
hole. From whence comes the collector
of thing? Then shell and boats, then
storehouse of the dead, then tomb of the

archives: eighteen locks, no key. All
songs must be sung to the fallen. Ghost
and harp: an occasion for celebration,
the litany begun, the guests disassembled
into sloppy baggage. Proffered the mask
of doubt, tongue of operetta, the gloves
of seduction, the noose of heaven. So one
cannot refuse to play dead, there or
then. Topography of terror: false cirrus
of snow off the peak. Body as oboe; wind
the soul. The coursed stone prison but a
hand before the eyes, a strap of steel
between the lips. To whom what then?
Celestial saddle? Necklace of teeth?
Chalice of redemption? Unrepentant
remorse? In daylight under the influence
of stars? Chaotic entropy: babel and
love: Always in catharsis, like a red
bird or a blue bird. Fugitive bird.
Echoic shoal as mordant of memory:
Often then, though the wish, nothing is
forgiven.

Tessitura of the Virgin

She grasps the raven's wing between her thighs.

The action creates color
juxtaposition, relation
of sex and flight
                    (flying),
possession
                              (ownership),
dismemberment,
poetic allusion,
symbology of pubic hair
to feathers,
apparent absence of hands,

or there are two women
and the above is wrong.

Then one is in possession
and the other is grasping
that possession, lesbian
connotations, cult fetish.

It is assumed the characters
are human, otherwise
there is a divergent progression
based on feline, canine . . .

Text exists in relation
to title.

Virgin is often associated
with Christianity and youth.
Then it could be heretical,
apocryphal. Edenic? Eve
absolved trespass.

The colors could be racial:
black on white, black on black.
Black on . . . :

chromatic symbols: dualism,
night and day;
or racist cant: black
flightless, possessed by sex;

attack on women: thighs
prevent flight.

Voice: range of the singer.

Labia, lips. What range
of singing, then? Virgins'
are unknown.

Has the raven been eaten,
discarded, buried, or immolated?

Or there are two women
and one is grasping the wing
with the thighs of the other.

Perhaps an opera piece.

Ravens consume carrion.
To enter pubic hair
is to enter a raven's gullet;
or pubic hair
has mastered the raven's
appetite.

Ravens croak, gargle,
they do not sing:
class statement.

"Grasp" is to hold securely,
not to fondle;
nakedness is implied,
though not explicit.

Beneath her tongue is an extracted fingernail.
:

Torture
Fascism
Cannibalism

Still two females: she and her?
Or one?:
Masochism.

Or the tortured.

Tongue implies speech.
So the fragment of hand
is an impediment.

To thought.

Censorship.

Tongue implies sex
so the fragment of hand
is a relic: finger
inserted.

Or ritual medication.
Rhinoceros horn.

Which her?

What would the polishing
on the fingernail be: Black?
White? Red?

Is the fingernail then
as a wafer?

Or drug?

Misspoken word?

I love her then as myself.

Love is easy.
Her is easier.

But do my possess self?

Which her?

It is possible for me
to collect her in my palms;
there is no weight;
in color she is tawny;
which her or she I am unsure:
I inhale her.

Then as myself appears
narcissistic, implosive.

Can I be projected onto,
or into, another,
like a bit of rooster spur,
bullet, or bone to be loved
in identity?

Probably.

If you feed the woman
every bite she eats, your hand
will be clothed as a puppet
in her image.

Which her?

Then implies time
and causality. Neither
of which are belief systems
of credibility.

And her name will be on her lips until I sing.

What shall the name be?
Love?
Mary?
Democracy?

I envision this as a tattoo.
The tongue gradually reducing
it, as everything, to nothing.

Femininity continues to divide,
plane off in a series
that is unnameable.

Are the lips painted otherwise?

I do not displace; to construct
an effigy now would be an act
of sacrifice
of which they are incapable.

They are then kissing;
if so, they are kissing
themselves.

Orality of voice
to cease the orality
of caress is unlikely
unless vocalization
includes practicable threats.

Which lips? If labial,
then tessiturial?

We will christen her: Hope

I will name I: Avarice

Ease

No

But I will sing only when she has written, in blood,
with her fingernail, the dead which will be joined,
on my back, so that I will know to whom I speak
when I am tired and unable to speak.

> At this point a cosmology
> is established;
> at least a landscape
> within which action can occur
> bearing some semblance
> to cognition.
>
> One in which both compression
> and expansion are possible,
> to include all souls,
> even disembodied, or embodied,
> which could conceivably occur.
>
> Fog is trite.
>
> An endless ocean
> would prohibit speech;
> endless air,
> prohibit place.
>
> Let's examine then the artifacts:
> a nail,
> a lip,
> a wing.
>
> A she,
> a her,
> an I.
>
> Temporality,
> spaciality.

Are these eight then enough
to create something?

Story or world?

between my lips is the raven's wing,
and though unable to sing, I still possess her tongue
to carefully grasp between her thighs.

I suppose.

Speech Runes Learn Thou,

        To Spite No One,

Least Out of Hate He Harm Thee

        These Wind Thou,

These Weave Thou,

        And Gather Them All Together

When Men To Moot

        Are Met At The Thing,

And All Thing – Men Are There

X:
it begins as a kind of unction; an anniversary

Narcosis:
stars are crossed wearing the vestments of despair
or its corollary, grief

Amnesia:
the reach is too pious, distance too empowered, too relief

(lips are estranged by speech)

at the heights of hope

Esthesia:
intransigent wounds that must be mute, cloistered

(there is nothing to be won,
no surreptitious coax,
no garner)

Fluxion:
the geometry of tilt equates yes with right, with west

Decadent:
you are unable to contain yourself

(you are unable to right
yourself)

Nocturne:
brief history, somnambulant architecture: dab and wattle

Sophism:
there is no factory in your body

Piquant:
efficacious tryst

Glissando:
you have memorized your apocryphal biography; seduced
by landscapes of vacuity; enamoured with broken bones

(denial)

Gnosis:
you can see with only the rods of the retina

(speak only in consonants)

Iris:
caution those that then are resplendent

Leaven:
armor of humor against hail of fracture

(switch hands)

(magnify the occasion of fall)

Oblivion:
the bondage of notion

(disappearance is your theme)

Trenchant:
you squander the gulf; augment the pile with precious:
that which dazzles deceives

(you probably understand:
the sanctuary levitates;
your version was invention)

Innominate:
a criminology replete with confiscations;
material symbols compulsively
on occasion sounds, like smoke's shadow

Hydra:
the celebration of your suffocation

(of, sweet nausea)

Inquisition:
contain this disintegration by refuting its cosmology;
sky blinding with animals

Quilt:
the world is spun in a thread of sound
beyond the range of hearing

(sacrifice)

Cant:
closure is enunciated at inception

Debauch:
there is no musician other than momentum
undesired presence

(the problem is not algebraic,
but love: how to collect
enough detritus to preclude
ascension; or enough light
to evade submergence)

((a kind of cheap purgation))

with enough change to squander in gender

Eviscerate:
every is arrayed and all faces possess name
enough articles of confusion

Key:
epistle bereft of presumed author
yet carried of his cadence
seasonal demarcation of reason

(or happenstance)

Milk:
the lacquered vase from which one drinks air:
grand theology of kaleidoscope

such winnowing as the pervasive ground cloud
dissipates into memory

           (classical suffering as vehicle
           of certainty: terminal doubt,
           temporal rift: tools
           for dislocating in space)

           ((coherence of movement prevents
           the conclusion of stasis))

           (harrier of thought;
           wanton release)

Catatonic:
oft the lute languished unclaimed to dancing
blurred vision, the aggregate map of vanity and its dross

           (possess you)

           ((in speech, in honor, in habit))

           (to thus be branded
           with the symbol of knowledge)

           ((all textures which you
           embrace as manifestation;
           all atonal laughters
           and brightening))

           (to walk out of enclosure
           is to walk into expanse,
           a certain vibrancy of form:
           snake vertebra or cornea)

((ideally there is no locus
of thing, only a habitual
pattern of occurrence,
or its semblance))

Flame:
cryogenic photograph as placard of healing

Ablate:
movement, even eyes, is prescribed
by received knowledge,
ark of retreat

Duress:
you water the long dead tree:
lazarus mechanistics
or quarantine

Replicate:
speech can be used to create a sphere
of exclusion around the soul,
as a bird, its nest, in swoop

> (I cannot stomach this seizure;
> denial of pleasure)

> ((there is no compassion,
> only the weight enfolding you
> like raptor wings))

Lacerate:
does appearance matter: without lips: without volition

> (seeing the room as animate,
> you are flight)

> ((the skull is magnetized
> toward falling))

(there is an aperture
in your mouth: sibling
of question; effigy of faith)

((of little matter,
though your hands are inked
with equations))

Y:
field of view has diminished to rapture:

Z:
(take this glass, this surmise)

((it will be the thing
you always cherish))

The Waltz

Euphoria (the transcendental odes: redemptive toward

blindness) Or at invisibility the ores, in violence

create a mirror: Meld toward identity — convexity through

acceleration (Like say kiss) Odor of carrion: lure

                                                    Thus

it began in infamy: the first step (an articulation):

accoutrement on the transformation To swirl into anonymity

Contraries resolved into an orchestra Appareled in a makeup

— to dissolve — shadows: posture then is meaning (Rapture

of tendon)

                        Skeleton juxtaposed with stone (bliss: no music

overlaid) Or the silk stockings: bliss The room fills

with fog (then transcend integrity) An abrupt gesture —

of fingers: transcription: treatise on red — the

thigh-elegance

                        You're dead, of course, (in this dance)

small objective: the lips are painted — oh, is the

equation — or the enclosing night (has been dreamt) before

the removal of taste (through taste)

Is choreographed

(then teleos) knowing of naught — the split (tongue)

slit Dance backward into disappearance (unknowing) Hospitality

of intoxication — down

Those allurements we (you) condescend

— to touch, out of hand, against — Being lost, within the

confinement (of ideal) flesh

The dreamt end (laughter

fragmenting — shards —) of the waltz, repository/

claustrophobia The white bird, its (elegant blood) beak

tempering The — voice — impassioned, temporal brevity

Spiritual collage:

harmonics, the residue (demonics) velvet

curtains, residual starlight (such light steps, such

destruction) The condition, reprieve

Caustic desire:

succulent fingertips (Predation — fur/Peace —

flaccidity) Ironic demonstrations of virtuosity; the

embracement of steps or walk

(You hope this never ends)

The swoon, incomparable flavor But transgress is confined —

or time in the dance — immalleable

Perhaps you have predicated

tune — turned seduction — beheaded (device of indifference)

or harpsichord time (vehicle of indelicacy) blue washed

into blue

Necessary time: blue washed into red, necessary

red: four/four time (to entice engagement one must feign

confusion)

Rending (fabric?) face, or a portrait, red

Voluptuous timidity is harvest: tacit — calendric disorientation

(compass)

(Now are you incarnate?) Moves are subtle (pain):

the nonredemptive: arc Hecate or somata — equivalencies

(correspondent)

Bewitched (disease) brain deflated: terse

consciousness — abnegated One, two One two or more ideas

of somnolence: glass head Jade tongue

No vocals, no

instruments: purity, carrion Music is distention

abbreviation of duration White teeth, ivory The blood

is liquor, flux

Or several lives: mutate: one Flurry

of hair, those perfumes: spite (against odoriferous

night) cadence

Transubstantial in the vigor (breasts) cadence

Translating tonal scale — derivation — (A vice of design)

Tongue to glass (You believe in the differences

of eyes, one absent)

Or the exterior romance (rain) as fetter

of nuance: not taste, against the greater backward

movement (cellar of potion) chance

Moves against the possessive

air: garment The tongue cannot remain within the mouth

(Speaking, ornamentation) against the stronger — design

of the inarticulate (novice desire): death's-head/xylophone

(curtsey and bow) C-sharp, C-flat

The Manichean Apology

I am god; there is no alternative hand.

Before my mother.
My face was a hand.

A face.

Six of clubs. Battery.

Battering the focus of one eye.

Astigmatic, as two voices
crossing at soprano.

Ambidextrous hands reveal
deceit twice.

I am the inventor of throw.
Naught.
Of *of.*

If three women assume
postures of devotion,
the third is left handed.

The mother of toss.

Suppose one possessed two hands.

You are then the articulator: zither.

If one is bisymmetical,
one is two.

But both eyes see nothing.
Nothing is last.

Nothing is bisymmetical.

Women's hands make them pregnant.

So music is responsible.
For night time.

Or an animal is killed.
Various postures.

These are exact mannequins.

Once smoke was blinding.
Because we believed it.

I am the collector of debt.
You owe your hands, your eyes,
your soul.

Wages; your error is fantasy.

Imagine yourself without hands
or without tongue.

Then you are complete.

I am the repository of forgiven vice.

We shall trade.
My hands for your signature;
my lips for your faith?

I could kill
but I am asleep,
designing structures
of doubt.

Easy: one eye is closed.

Corruption and decay are causal:
I walk backward.

Once there was the capacity
to grasp simple concepts.

Like right.

Once there was a formula
to determine the growth
of geodes: progressive
absence as source.

This is pure entrapment.

All right, I am the two of hearts.

I am not you.

You neither enter,
nor become,
light here.

Here: a vague coaxiation
of blue and desire.

Gather the threads of the garment,
therein lies, perhaps, water.

Siege: you are eroded by light.

No. You are an apology.

Light erodes light.

A template? A vendetta?
A faith.

"you" is a euphemism for "condition"

"light" is a euphemism for "fragmentation"

There is no memory involved;
there is no involved.

The Sun?

Putrefaction.

Once the light absolves
you you begin to enter you,
you.

A mountain of flint
does not disclose, enclose.

Sublime distress: call
it posture; call.

So what warrants deaffirmation?
Are the blossoms then projections
of your desire; artifacts
of delight, or of light?

All right, there is the trace
of a tree.

Or of a beckoning.

All right, there is a residue.

Wood grain splits longitudinally.
That is a matter of light.

Fire.

In each fist there inhabits
a reluctance.

A reluctance of speech.

Then the earth craved sustenance.

To face west is to solicit death.
North: efficacious
architecture of dust.

Clouds contrive.

It is a racial habit to move
rock: edifice = buffoonery = aquaduct
= tomb = X.

Why affirm that stone
is tangible light?

You are a miser of light.

"you" is a euphemism for "light"

The scattered feathers.

The feathers scattered.

The great reluctance.

Single trains of behavior:
lift and place;
light and place.

I am slowly dearticulating into soil.

"I" is a euphemism for "soil"

You are the light; you are a
way.

In the sea there is a valley
of corpses.
Navigation is by darkness.

The compass
does not invert light.

All this is comprised
by a gesture.

One which says, I am blind.

Artifacts of age
deteriorate in light.

The feathers scattered.

The eyes as recipients
of light are thus destroyed.

There is no one to whom
this gesture is appropriate.

"no one" is a euphemism for "light"

Is music then light
to our ears?

I have moved a thousand
clods of earth. Still
the earth is unmoved.

Who then lied
the relation of fire
to light?

"who" is a euphemism for "you"

The water conspires
the corpses; the darkness
purifies the light.

"corpse" is a euphemism for "tomorrow"

All right, both hands are empty.

"empty" is a euphemism for "armed"

All right, both eyes are blind.

"blind" is a euphemism for "the eyes
are the windows of the soul"

"soul" is a euphemism for "light"

"windows" is a euphemism for "water"

"water" is a euphemism for "you"

"you" is a euphemism for "I"

"I" exists only as euphemism:

"I" have lied throughout;
I was mistaken.

Government of Rhapsody

naught enters, naught
exits clasped
to horoscopes
of its persuasion, purpose
and praise
that which does not confirm
redolence
which emptiness necessitates

undernamed
into plurality, flocks
spared discretions
of air, topographic lapses
deflecting sunlight
to cast memory shadows

prematurely rent by occasions
of sound
though impetus of flight
is condoned
by sight: hawk shadow
boomerang spun
not to hand
but night

all strictures of shout
and voice timid
vibration victim
of diffusion even
of breath, even
of string

councils of weight
against which to rancor
like catholicism
of botany or turbulent
collapse of noon
about boulders
scriven with entreaties
against confines of mortal

sleep then with flawless
destiny enunciating syllables
of blood from an era
forbidden trespass
denied monarchy over
congregated flux

flesh rapture but antique
cautiously born
through categories
of disintent, oblique
scanting of precipitous decline

four winds converge
into demonics, spit
the air against
theft of garment
or soul

what broods internal
cast into finality, metallurgy
of chalice
blade, gnosis
of flame
against fire

fruit falls with equal
indifference affixed
to unseen benign
fluster submerged
against will

deflected, damned
unconscious to happenstance
of correction, ghost
of wisp or incrimination
by glance

trembled into long
falling, sight of sea
eroding into color, darkness
into falling
fast out
of one's self
toward what all withers

cast awaver tremulous
web alight
in spring bearing blind
anticipating harbor
against drift, chance
collision

wanton ridden, rife
with diversion, compass
and dull, dumb love
smeared like light
on walls

gap compressed
by desire tilted askance
squandering elite debacles
of utterance grafted
like tissue onto
occasion, onto
celebration

forgiveness, shroud
of air forever placid, remuneration
against paid debt
of despair, device
for issuance
into sleep, or refuge
from trust in surface

tangled formulas back
into themselves, severing foliage
assigned to mask
truant calibration
of feature, face
and temerity

humor of homicide
with those of rancid
articulation disposed
to ideation extant
in only that which prepares
offal for glamor

into abject
darkness of eyes, brilliance
of skin, coffin
of lips, listing toward severance
of self, bells
magic bells
do not redeem

batten the brain, there
is no reticence in rock
that in which there is nothing
to squander, savor
collect like figments
of life: the toys
do lie unheard
yet malicious shit
about governance of pain

music does not cease
sequestered somnolence:
there resides
no residence amenable
to disease; any wall
walls

graft thus dissident hope
upon space, neither
the room
neither the shadow
of your arm
reaching shade

no garlands were exuded
nor temperance taught: prize
corpse anointed
in juncture with lemon
honey
judicious exaltation
of word prize
of tongued

sweet death release those wizened
traits surfaced as need
into voiced person graft
what spaciousness attends
within skull
surfeit of trust;
be you now

in violation
of the species of meaning
prescribed by nobility
oration toward when hope
squanders throws
of youth

succulants clasp at travail
do mean exaltation
after sustenance, chance
before unhappy ending
as ships tap
docks, metronome
of unlistening

no veiling: as
in world
dismembered, to be eaten
in static brilliance

Geisha Mime

. . . . a mute soliloquy that the phantom, white as a yet unwritten page, holds in both face and gesture at full length to his soul.

— Mallarmé

Beneath kaoline, the skin is damascus. Death
or ceramics; the image is frangible, entity.
Love as a magnetic enclosure, white water
dissipated beyond mirroring face.

Reflection is a path, labyrinth of recedings,
toward and against desire, as when one walks
backward toward lust; or knives as door,
odor as warning.

Her mouth is wet with stars; the curve of her
waist is inevitable failure, acquiescence.

You hold yourself in your own arms and are enamoured
to have become the pretense. Or you are her.
Or her pretense.

Opulent forests. Decay. And mannerisms.

You clothe your skin in skin. Hallucinating oblique
passions antecedent to dawn, great flavor of blood.
Or illuminated eyes, flammable dance,
at the delicacy of insight.

Your hands are retroactive calendars; she is a drawing
in charcoal on rock.

Ocean waves are not random: predestination. As gifts
enameled thighs can be returned.

When in a specific perfume, your body is displaced,
or dismembered.

Or flesh is brocade. At birth
they bind the face to compel neoteny.

Mirror or lithography. What she puts in her mouth.
Conceptualizing reproduction. Or moonlight and frost,
which in walking you find is a lake.

Lace gloves and aggregate collapse.

Seven versions of the face, all face in control.
To police the singing, abandon the way. Syphilitic
grin: ecstatics define vibration.

Define dissonant appetite: she takes off her hands
with her gloves; misplaces her tongue.

To exist only as print or light. Painting of light
where she puts her tongue in her mouth: speech
or sustenance.

Lace is frost. The tremors are kinetic: dissipation
of heat and orgasm; the heart is painted on the thigh,
lips painted on the mirror:

Amputation of name.

You are permitted to define that which is beautiful.

The fluent absences. All in the eyes.

There is a great vertical wind which attempts to elongate
and separate you from earth. Porcelain. A breast. Wheat.

Her asymmetrical body: gravity, moon. One black iris bleeding
horizontally into her hairline, cartography: lies.

Pursued by a storm, memory; indices replicating
each, twisting pore, follicle, track of spittle
down the bereaved occasion of your smoke, hold

your fragmenting grace, slit, lick absence

in which you wash your face clean of semblance:

a porcelain breast as bowl, filled with milk: white

as absence of color. No, confers the non-iconic
nacreous laughter.

Colonnade of painted spruce. Laceration of space,
or the value of weapons. Impaled. Feral intimacy:
cloven and seizure. *The painted snow.*

Red intimacy: *painted mist.*

Structure defined, behavior articulated: representation
to compel emotion: harelip with tines, impassioned hair,
horse and violet sky; *in the painting,*
the painting.

Frozen swoon. Ceramics to portray disease. The balance
of white to black: nothingness in every corner.
The current cannot flow; revelers do not swallow.

In tiny strokes the ocean occurs on the eyes. *Painted
hallucination:* stars in the hair.

In the painting, she holds a paintbrush; licking
the hairs to define the eyelashes,

or a needle impaling alphabet into flesh.

(In the mirror, the lithograph depicts a man
reading his future from the entrails of a pig.)

Glass skirt. Voyeur exile. Blue silicate or obsidian.
That which is beneath That which is inside That which fills:
kaolin That which is or is idea.

Skirt Glass: sustenance

to what eye? Mercantile dice? Mendicant poker?

A state

dependant on optics: voluptuous convexity, telescoping
impassioned.

The skirt is a perfume bottle? (Olfactory optics)

Optics of synesthesia. Or your hand in . . .

Or your hand in

water. Or your hand in darkness. In snow.

But within

the glass skirt is a perfect vacuum? Dearticulated
skeleton?
Sleeping in a goat mask to offend death:

Red lips suspended in a glass of ice:

Black hair as camouflage:

Cleansing blood from genitals with milk:

Gold ring through the lip:

The bedroom ceiling painted with nightmares:

Concealed in a block of air:

Seeing through flammable sustenance:

(In your — her — final disappearance
what then will saturate the space
so abandoned, orphaned of flesh —
the damascus, the brocade — other
than breath — kaoline — or desire?)

Emptiness is then empty of emptiness:
Costume.

Phillip Foss

Phillip Foss is the author of eight previous volumes of poetry, *Roaoring Fork Passage, Grace; The Snakes and the Dogs, Yana, House of Eagles, Somata, The Composition of Glass, The Excesses The Caprices,* and *Courtesan of Seizure.*

Additionally, he founded the literary magazine, *Tyuonyi,* and edited the anthology, *The Clouds Threw This Light: Contemporary Native American Poetry.* With Charles Bernstein, he edited *Patterns / Contexts / Time : A Symposium on Contemporary Poetry* and with Stacy Doris and Emmanuel Hocquard, he edited, *Violence of the White Page: Contemporary French Poetry.*

He is the founder of the Creatrive Writing Program at the Institute of American Indian Arts in Santa Fe, and currently is the Executive Director of the Health Resource Center of New Mexico, where he lives with his wife and two children.

Other Books from Chax Press